MW00379069

Essential Que
How are offspring like their parents?

Animal Families

by Deborah November

Many animals live in families.
They take care of their
babies.

Deer mothers feed their babies. Soon the **young** deer can eat grass.

Baby deer have **spots**.
The spots help them hide
in the grass.

antlers

Adult deer grow big.
Boy deer grow antlers.

Kangaroos take care of their young, too. Young kangaroos are called joeys.

pouch

A joey lives in its mother's
pouch.

Kangaroos cannot walk.
But they can hop!

This baby lives in a pouch, too. It is a koala. Its mother **grooms** its **fur**.

Penguin parents work together. Father penguins watch the eggs.

Baby penguins come out of the eggs. Then the mother keeps the babies warm.

baby alligator

egg

Alligators lay lots of eggs.

The mother alligator carries her babies. She **protects** them.

Baby alligators are small.
They can grow a **foot** every
year. Then they are big!

Animals take care of their babies. They are family.

Respond to Reading

Summarize

Tell about *Animal Families*. You may use the chart.

Main Topic		
Detail	Detail	Detail

Text Evidence

1. How do deer take care of their babies? Main Topic and Key Details

2. Reread page 5. Look at the picture. What does the word *antlers* mean? Vocabulary

3. Write about how alligators take care of their babies. Write About Reading

Compare Texts
Read about how tadpoles
become frogs.

Tadpoles into Frogs

Frogs begin
as eggs.

When the egg hatches, the tadpole is born.

These babies look like fish.

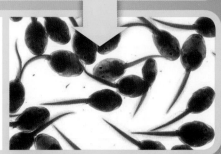

Tadpoles have a tail, a mouth, and gills to breathe.

gills

mouth

tail

They grow legs.

The tadpole's tail goes away.

The tadpole is a frog! He hops out of the water.

Make Connections

How are tadpoles like frogs?

Essential Question

How are the baby animals In *Animal Families* like the tadpole?

Text to Text

19

Focus on
Science

Purpose To find out how baby animals are like their parents

What to Do

Step 1 Work with a partner. Choose one animal from this book.

Step 2 Draw a picture of the animal as a baby.

Step 3 Then draw the animal as an adult.

Conclusion Talk about how the baby is different from the adult.